How Not To Suck At Managing Your Money

Bruce Hoyt

Published by Four Aces Publishing LLC, 2026.

HOW NOT TO SUCK AT MANAGING YOUR MONEY

First edition. August 15, 2026.

ISBN: 979-8905999512

Written by Bruce Hoyt.

Table of Contents

Reader Note 1
Preface 2
Contents 3
Introduction: Stop Trying to Win With Willpower 4
The Decision Loop 8
Money Scripts 11
State Before Strategy 14
Defaults and Friction 18
Spending That Fits 21
Decision Hygiene 24
Three Kinds of Risk 28
Time Buckets and Continuity 32
A Personal Investment Constitution 35
Information Boundaries 40
Transition Mode 44
The Review System 47
Conclusion: A System You Can Trust 51
Appendix: The Money by Design Toolkit 53
Bonus Section 58
Selected References 70
About the Author 75

Reader Note

This book is for education and reflection. It is not individualized financial, investment, tax, legal, or mental-health advice. Financial products, laws, tax rules, and personal circumstances change. Consider consulting qualified professionals before making decisions with significant consequences.

The people in this book are composites created to make ideas concrete. Names, occupations, dollar amounts, and circumstances have been fictionalized. They are not claims about identifiable clients, and no vignette should be read as a promise that a particular strategy will produce the same result for someone else.

This book explores the practical intersection of behavior, decision-making, and personal finance, with a focus on turning sound intentions into systems that can survive ordinary emotion and real-life change.

Preface

Let's face it, almost everyone at some point in their lives has sucked at managing their money. Count me in that group too. But as we get older, we try to learn from our mistakes and put ourselves in a better position for the future. This book is about the mistakes we make and how to make a plan to avoid them going forwards. Most suggestions here could be considered obvious, yet we don't do them without conscious effort and we don't implement them into an intelligent plan. My hope though is that everyone reading this implements a few of these suggestions and turns their money management life around!

> *"The investor's chief problem—and even his worst enemy—is likely to be himself."* — ***Benjamin Graham***

Contents

Introduction: Stop Trying to Win With Willpower
Part I — Understand Your Financial Operating System
1. The Decision Loop
2. Money Scripts
3. State Before Strategy
Part II — Design the Environment
4. Defaults and Friction
5. Spending That Fits
6. Decision Hygiene
Part III — Build a Plan You Can Continue
7. Three Kinds of Risk
8. Time Buckets and Continuity
9. A Personal Investment Constitution
Part IV — Stay Adaptive
10. Information Boundaries
11. Transition Mode
12. The Review System
Conclusion: A System You Can Trust
Appendix: The Money by Design Toolkit
Bonus Section
Glossary
Selected References
About the Author

Introduction: Stop Trying to Win With Willpower

"The future is inherently uncertain and financial markets are inherently unpredictable."

— George Soros

Most financial plans are written as if a calm, rested, fully informed person will execute them forever.

That person does not exist.

Real decisions happen while a child is sick, a market is falling, a colleague has just announced a promotion, or a phone is serving an advertisement engineered to turn longing into urgency. They happen after a poor night's sleep and before a difficult conversation. A plan can be mathematically sound and still fail because it was built for a decision-maker who never gets frightened, distracted, lonely, proud, or tired.

This is why knowing more does not automatically change what you do. Knowledge matters. It helps you detect fees, compare tradeoffs, understand interest, and recognize risk. But knowledge is only one component in a larger system. The other components include the state of your body, the story you attach to an event, the options your environment makes easy, and the rules you prepared before the pressure arrived.

The premise of this book is simple: **better financial behavior is usually a design problem before it is a discipline problem.**

Think about Elena, a composite of several familiar situations. She earns enough to save. She has read books about investing and has a retirement account at work. Every few months, however, she moves money into savings and then pulls it back out. A stressful week ends in a costly weekend. An anxious headline leads her to pause retirement contributions. A raise creates three new recurring expenses. She concludes that she lacks self-control.

Her conclusion is too harsh and not especially useful. Elena's money moves through an unexamined loop:

1. A cue appears: stress, comparison, opportunity, bad news.

2. Her physical and emotional state gives that cue urgency.

3. She tells herself a story: *I deserve this, I am falling behind*, or *I need to act now*.

4. The environment presents an easy action: tap, transfer, sell, subscribe.

5. The immediate consequence, relief, excitement, safety, rewards the action.

The result is not random. The system is producing exactly what it was built to produce.

Change the system and different behavior becomes possible. Elena can learn to recognize the cue. She can label her state before making a decision. She can add a waiting period to purchases that become tempting under stress. She can automate saving for the day after payday. She can write rules for market declines while markets are quiet. She can review her choices without turning the review into a trial of her character.

None of these changes requires her to become fearless. They make fear less authoritative.

The five layers of a money decision

Throughout this book, we will work with five layers:

- **Signal:** What happened? A bill arrived, a price moved, a friend bought something, or income changed.

- **State:** What condition are you in? Calm, rushed, depleted, excited, ashamed, or threatened.

- **Story:** What meaning did you assign? Stories turn facts into identities and forecasts.

- **Structure:** What does your environment make easy, difficult, automatic, visible, or invisible?

- **Review:** How will you learn from the result without relying on memory or blame?

The five layers explain why the same person can behave differently in two nearly identical situations. They also show where to intervene. Sometimes the most useful change is intellectual: correct a false belief. Sometimes it is environmental: remove a card from a shopping account. Sometimes it is procedural: require a second review before a large transfer. Sometimes it is emotional: recognize that a decision made to end discomfort is not necessarily a decision that advances a goal.

The chapters are organized around building a complete operating system rather than touring a catalog of interesting money stories. Part I helps you see the internal machinery. Part II changes the setting in which choices are made. Part III converts goals into a durable plan. Part IV creates protocols for noise, disruption, and revision.

You will not be asked to predict markets or eliminate emotion. You will be asked to make fewer important decisions in improvised conditions.

That distinction matters. A good system does not guarantee a painless life or a perfect result. It reduces the number of preventable errors, creates room to recover, and keeps one frightened afternoon from overruling years of careful work.

Before continuing, write one sentence:

The money behavior I most want to understand is ___________.

Do not write the behavior you think sounds responsible. Write the one that creates friction in your actual life: avoiding statements, spending after conflict, changing investments after news, keeping too much cash, rescuing relatives at your own expense, or refusing to spend even when a purchase is affordable and valuable.

That behavior is not your identity. It is evidence. This book will teach you how to read it.

PART I

Understand Your Financial Operating System

The Decision Loop

A choice begins before the choice

"Far more money has been lost by investors preparing for corrections, or trying to anticipate corrections, than has been lost in corrections themselves." — ***Peter Lynch***

Nina opened her investment app while waiting for a meeting to start. She had no decision scheduled. She was not checking progress toward a goal. She was filling ninety seconds.

The account was down sharply for the day. A banner linked to a story about a possible recession. By the time the meeting began, Nina had moved a third of her long-term portfolio into cash.

If she later described the event as "I decided to reduce risk," the sentence would hide most of what happened. The decision began with boredom, proximity, a red number, an alarming headline, and the ability to trade immediately. The explanation arrived after the action.

Research on "risk as feelings" describes how emotional reactions can diverge from cognitive assessments of probability and consequence (Loewenstein et al., 2001). In plain language, what feels dangerous can dominate what you previously concluded was acceptable. The feeling is real. It is not, by itself, a complete risk analysis.

A useful model is:

Cue → State → Story → Action → Aftermath

The loop can run in seconds. A restaurant invitation produces social pressure; fatigue makes refusal feel costly; the story becomes *I cannot be the difficult one*; the card comes out; relief follows. Or a bonus appears, excitement expands what seems normal, the story becomes *this is my new level*, and a one-time payment turns into a permanent monthly obligation.

The aftermath matters because it trains the next decision. If buying ends discomfort, the brain learns that buying is a fast route to relief. If checking an account reduces uncertainty for a moment, checking becomes easier to repeat, even when it increases anxiety over time.

Capture the loop, not the verdict

People often review a choice by asking whether it was good or bad. That question is too blunt. A profitable investment can come from a reckless process. A sensible decision can have a disappointing outcome. If you judge only the result, luck becomes a teacher and may teach the wrong lesson.

Use a decision record for choices that are expensive, hard to reverse, or emotionally charged. It can fit on one page:

- What happened immediately before I wanted to act?
- What did I notice in my body and mood?
- What sentence made the action seem necessary?
- What alternatives did I consider?
- What did I expect to happen, and by when?
- What would make this choice reversible?

Do not write a legal brief. Two minutes is enough. The goal is to preserve information that memory will later polish away.

Consider Andre, who repeatedly replaced working electronics. His explanation was that he valued quality. A month of decision records revealed a narrower pattern: the urge was strongest after professional criticism. The purchase was not mainly about the device. It restored a feeling of competence.

That insight did not require Andre to swear off technology. It gave him more options. When the cue appeared, he could wait, repair, rent, or choose a different way to address the injury. The purchase became a choice rather than a reflex with a receipt.

Separate the layers

When a loop is active, facts and stories blur. Separate them deliberately.

Signal: "The account is down 8 percent this month."

State: "I am tense and have checked it six times today."

Story: "This decline proves I was foolish and must prevent further damage."

Structure: "The trading app is on my home screen and has no delay."

Review: "My written plan says this money is for a goal fifteen years away and calls for a scheduled allocation review, not a response to a monthly decline."

The story may eventually prove correct; perhaps circumstances truly changed. But separating it from the signal prevents a forecast from masquerading as an observed fact.

Design practice: the seven-day map

For seven days, record one money impulse each day. It may be a purchase, avoidance, transfer, account check, or urge to give advice. Capture the five parts of the loop. At the end of the week, circle repeated cues and repeated forms of relief.

Then finish this sentence:

When __________ happens, I tend to tell myself __________, which leads me to __________ because it gives me __________ right away.

You have not solved the behavior yet. You have done something more important: you have located it.

Money Scripts

The rules you absorbed before you chose them

"Investing should be more like watching paint dry or watching grass grow. If you want excitement, take $800 and go to Las Vegas." — ***Paul Samuelson***

Families teach money long before they explain it. A child notices whether bills are opened or hidden, whether wealthy people are admired or distrusted, whether gifts repair conflict, whether asking about money is rude, and whether security means cash in a drawer or confidence that more income can be earned.

Research on financial socialization finds that parents, work, and education all contribute to young adults' financial knowledge, attitudes, and behavior (Shim et al., 2010). Research on money beliefs has also identified recurring clusters of beliefs associated with different financial patterns (Klontz et al., 2011). These findings do not mean childhood seals a financial fate. They mean old rules may keep operating after the original conditions disappear.

Luis grew up in a household where a late bill could trigger a crisis. As an adult, he built a stable career and accumulated substantial cash, yet investing felt irresponsible. His rule was not "cash has a lower expected return." It was "available cash keeps catastrophe away." That rule had once been adaptive. Applied without limit, it made every long-term decision feel unsafe.

Maya learned a different rule. In her family, visible generosity proved loyalty. She paid relatives' expenses even when doing so increased her own high-interest debt. Saying no felt less like a budget decision than a betrayal.

The numbers alone cannot resolve either situation. First, the rule has to become visible.

Four questions that expose a script

Instead of assigning yourself a permanent type, investigate the rules behind specific behavior.

1. **What did money mean in my household?** Safety, power, secrecy, love, virtue, conflict, possibility, or something else?

2. **What happened to people who had more?** Were they respected, resented, recruited, feared, or expected to rescue everyone?

3. **Which financial behavior earned approval?** Saving, earning, giving, displaying, sacrificing, avoiding debt, or never asking for help?

4. **What was never discussed?** Income, bills, investing, inheritance, addiction, unemployment, or mistakes?

Write answers as observations, not accusations. The purpose is not to place your family on trial. People often transmit rules that helped them survive their own circumstances.

From inherited rule to chosen policy

A script is broad and absolute:

Debt is always shameful.

A policy is specific and conditional:

I will not use high-interest consumer debt for lifestyle spending. I may consider fixed-rate debt for a durable asset when the payment fits my cash-flow limits and I understand the total cost.

A script says:

If I can afford it, I should provide it.

A policy says:

I have a defined annual amount for family support. I do not borrow to give, and I do not commit during an emergency phone call.

Policies are easier to examine because they state a scope, a trigger, and a boundary. They can be revised without declaring your past self foolish.

The loyalty conflict

Changing a money rule can feel disloyal. A first-generation professional may experience saving as abandonment when relatives need help. A person raised in scarcity may experience enjoyment as carelessness. Someone from a high-spending environment may fear that a simpler life announces failure.

The solution is not to insult the old rule. Thank it for the problem it was trying to solve, then update it.

Luis revised "cash prevents catastrophe" into three policies: maintain a defined emergency reserve, invest only money not needed for near-term obligations, and review the allocation twice a year. The reserve honored the need for safety. The limit prevented safety from consuming every other goal.

Maya created a family-support account funded automatically. Requests above the balance required a forty-eight-hour pause and a conversation with her partner. Generosity remained part of her identity; improvisation stopped controlling it.

Design practice: the script audit

Complete these prompts quickly:

- People with money are __________.
- The safest place for money is __________.
- Spending on myself means __________.
- If someone I love needs money, I must __________.
- A financial mistake proves __________.

Choose the sentence with the strongest emotional charge. Ask: *Where did I learn this? What problem was it meant to solve? In what situations is it still useful? Where does it now create harm?*

Rewrite it as a policy with a limit and a review date.

The goal is not to become a person without a money story. It is to become the editor of the story you use.

State Before Strategy

The same plan, a different nervous system

A budget didn't limit my freedom. It actually gave me freedom!" — ***Rachel Cruze***

Owen reviewed his budget on two Sundays. On the first, he had slept well, eaten, and finished a walk. He cut an unused subscription, scheduled a transfer, and closed the laptop in twenty minutes. On the second, he was exhausted after an argument. He stared at the same categories, declared the entire plan impossible, and ordered an expensive dinner.

The spreadsheet did not change. The decision-maker's state did.

Under emotional arousal, people can struggle to predict how they will think and act in a cooler state, and the reverse is also true. This "hot-cold empathy gap" appears across many kinds of decisions. Related work shows that feelings can shape perceptions of risk separately from cognitive evaluation (Loewenstein et al., 2001).

This does not mean every uncomfortable feeling invalidates a decision. It means state should be treated as information. A racing heart, narrowed attention, or urgent need for relief reduces the range of options you can see.

Green, amber, red

Create three decision states.

Green: You are rested enough, not under immediate pressure, and can explain the choice in writing. Normal decisions may proceed.

Amber: You are rushed, angry, euphoric, ashamed, or depleted. You may gather information and prepare options, but delay large or irreversible actions.

Red: You are in acute crisis, panic, intoxication, sleep deprivation, or conflict. Protect essentials. Do not make discretionary commitments, major purchases, or unscheduled portfolio changes.

The thresholds should be concrete. "Large" could mean any unplanned expense above $500, or a percentage of monthly take-home pay. "Irreversible" may include signing a lease, lending money, resigning, selling a concentrated asset, or accepting a product you do not understand.

The rule is not "never decide while emotional." Life does not offer that luxury. The rule is "match the decision to the state." In red, pay for urgent medical care and secure housing. Do not redesign your retirement plan because the urge to act is unbearable.

A state reset is not avoidance

Delay works only when it has an endpoint. "I will deal with this later" is avoidance. "I will review this tomorrow at 10 a.m. after sleep, with the account documents open" is a protocol.

A short reset may include food, sleep, movement, a conversation with a neutral person, or twenty minutes away from a screen. The purpose is not to manufacture optimism. It is to restore enough cognitive range to compare options.

Implementation-intention research shows the usefulness of linking an anticipated situation to a preselected response, an if-then plan (Gollwitzer, 1999). A financial version might be:

If I want to make an unscheduled investment change after consuming market news, then I will record the proposed change and wait until the next morning before submitting it.

Or:

If a purchase above $300 feels necessary because I had a bad day, then I will place it on a list and reconsider it after forty-eight hours.

The power comes from deciding the response before the cue arrives.

Build a decision bench

Some choices are too consequential to make alone, but advice is useful only if the people involved have roles. Build a small "decision bench":

- a technical expert for taxes, law, insurance, or investments;
- a grounded person who understands your values and will ask uncomfortable questions;
- a partner or household member affected by the decision.

One person may fill more than one role. Avoid appointing someone whose only qualification is confidence.

When asking for help, bring a question rather than an emotion disguised as a question. Instead of "Tell me this will be okay," ask, "Which assumptions would have to fail for this plan to become unsafe?" Instead of "Should I sell?" ask, "Has my goal, time horizon, liquidity need, or agreed allocation changed?"

Design practice: write your pause rule

Choose one recurring high-stakes situation. Define:

- the cue that moves you into amber or red;
- the actions that are prohibited in that state;
- the protective actions that remain allowed;
- the exact time and conditions for reconsideration;
- the person, document, or policy you will consult.

Put the rule where the action occurs. A pause rule hidden in a notebook cannot compete with a trading button on your phone.

Your state will always influence your financial life. The objective is not to remove it. The objective is to stop confusing urgency with authority.

PART II

Design the Environment

Defaults and Friction

Your environment is already voting

"Don't look for the needle in the haystack. Just buy the haystack." —***John C. Bogle***
Many people describe saving as a monthly act of virtue. In practice, saving often loses because spending has better infrastructure. The card is stored. The app remembers the address. The subscription renews without a decision. Savings, by contrast, requires opening an account, choosing an amount, remembering a date, and tolerating the feeling that the money is no longer available.

This is not a fair contest.

Defaults matter because people frequently remain with a preselected option. In a widely cited study of 401(k) plans, automatic enrollment substantially increased participation, while many participants retained the default contribution rate and investment allocation (Madrian & Shea, 2001). Defaults do not eliminate choice. They determine which choice happens when no new action is taken.

Your financial life contains defaults whether you designed them or not:

- where income lands;
- which bills are paid automatically;
- what happens to a raise;
- whether a credit card number is stored;
- which account appears first when you open an app;
- how frequently you see investment performance;
- whether a purchase requires one step or six.

If your goals depend on repeatedly defeating those defaults, the environment is stronger than the plan.

Make the desired path ordinary

Start with recurring decisions. Each one is a chance for interruption, forgetting, or renegotiation. Automation can turn a chosen policy into a default.

Priya wanted to save 12 percent of take-home pay but transferred whatever remained at month's end. There was rarely much left. She changed the sequence: income arrived, an automatic transfer moved money to savings the following morning, and spending adjusted to the remainder. The total income did not change. The default did.

Automation should not be blind. A transfer that regularly causes an overdraft is not a successful system. Begin with an amount the cash flow can support, monitor the first few cycles, and set a low-balance alert. A system must be durable enough to survive ordinary variation.

The Save More Tomorrow program offers another design principle: people committed in advance to directing part of future raises toward retirement saving (Thaler & Benartzi, 2004). The broader lesson is useful even outside workplace plans. A future increase can be assigned before lifestyle expectations absorb it.

Write a raise rule now:

When take-home pay increases, ___ percent of the increase will go to long-term goals, ___ percent to near-term goals, and the remainder may support current life.

The percentages are personal. The advance decision is the important part.

Use friction selectively

Friction is anything that adds time, effort, visibility, or a second decision. It is not automatically good. Add it before impulsive or high-consequence actions; remove it before repetitive beneficial actions.

To add friction:

- remove stored payment details;
- disable one-click purchasing;
- keep long-term savings at a separate institution;
- require a household conversation above a set amount;
- move trading applications off the phone;
- use a waiting list instead of a shopping cart;
- prohibit new subscriptions until one existing subscription is canceled.

To remove friction:

- automate bills and savings where cash flow is reliable;
- keep a short checklist for recurring reviews;
- store beneficiary and insurance information in one organized place;
- preselect the account used for planned giving;
- schedule appointments before a deadline becomes urgent.

The best design is asymmetric: easy in the direction you have chosen, slower in the direction you tend to regret.

Beware of hostile convenience

Convenience is not neutral. Businesses remove friction when doing so increases completion. The countdown timer, buy-now-pay-later button, free trial, and automatic renewal are design choices. They may be useful, but they shift the burden of resistance to you.

Treat urgency claims as requests to suspend your process. Sometimes urgency is real: a tax deadline, a limited insurance enrollment period, or an expiring contractual right. Verify the deadline outside the sales interface. A retailer's timer is not the same as a legal deadline.

Design practice: the friction audit

Draw two columns. In the first, list three actions you want to happen more often. In the second, list three actions you want to happen less often. For every item, count the steps required today.

Then make one desired action one step easier and one regretted action one step harder. Do not redesign your whole financial life at once. Environmental changes compound through repetition; a small improvement attached to every payday can matter more than a dramatic system you abandon in a month.

Spending That Fits

A budget is an allocation of life

*"The key to dealing with the future lies in knowing where you are, even if you can't know precisely where you're going." — **Howard Marks***

Spending is often discussed as if there were two categories: responsible and wasteful. That language invites shame and hides the real question. Money is exchanged for time, comfort, access, identity, care, beauty, status, mobility, and possibility. The task is to determine which exchanges actually improve your life and which merely create a brief change in feeling.

Keisha's bank statement looked disciplined. She saved aggressively, avoided debt, and rarely spent on leisure. It also revealed a pattern of takeout, rush shipping, and late fees during weeks when she worked excessive hours. Her "frivolous spending" was partly the price of a schedule with no margin.

A stricter dining budget would have treated the symptom. A better analysis asked whether she could buy back time more intentionally, reduce preventable fees, and preserve the forms of leisure she genuinely valued.

Satisfaction is personal, but it can be observed

Research has found that people often report greater happiness from experiential purchases than material purchases, although the categories overlap and individual circumstances matter (Van Boven & Gilovich, 2003). Other work found an association between well-being and spending that fit the buyer's personality, with an experiment providing evidence that personality-matched spending could affect positive emotion (Matz et al., 2016). Neither finding creates a universal shopping rule. A musical instrument may be a possession that enables years of meaningful experience. An expensive trip may be miserable if it expresses someone else's idea of a good life.

The practical move is to measure your own satisfaction.

For one month, mark discretionary purchases with two quick ratings:

- **Anticipated value:** How good did I expect this to be, from 1 to 5?

- **Remembered value:** Two weeks later, how much value did it actually provide, from 1 to 5?

Add one word describing the value: connection, convenience, mastery, recovery, status, novelty, beauty, or obligation.

Patterns emerge quickly. Some purchases are exciting in anticipation and nearly invisible afterward. Others look ordinary on the statement but support daily life repeatedly.

Distinguish pleasure, relief, and repair

Pleasure is not a problem. But three forms of spending can look identical at checkout:

- **Pleasure:** I expect to enjoy this and can afford it within my plan.
- **Relief:** I want this purchase to end a feeling right now.
- **Repair:** I hope this purchase will change how I am seen, restore self-worth, or settle a conflict.

Relief and repair are not automatically forbidden. A hotel room during a family emergency may be both relief and necessity. The distinction matters because the promised outcome is different. A purchase may successfully provide comfort while failing to solve the loneliness, resentment, or insecurity assigned to it.

Before an unplanned purchase, ask: *What job am I hiring this money to do?* If the job is emotional repair, name a second way to address the same need. You may still buy. You will be less likely to demand that the purchase accomplish what no object can reliably do.

Build a values floor, not only a spending ceiling

Traditional budgets set maximums. A values-based plan may also set minimums. If relationships matter, reserve money for shared meals or travel before the month becomes crowded. If health matters, fund preventive care or an activity you will actually use. If learning matters, create a modest education account.

A values floor prevents every meaningful expense from feeling like a failure of restraint. It also exposes false values. If "creativity" appears on every values exercise but receives neither time nor money for a year, it may be an admired idea rather than a current priority. That is not a moral problem. It is useful information.

Mental accounts: tool and trap

People commonly group money into mental accounts by source or purpose (Thaler, 1999). This can help: a separate repair fund protects money for an irregular but predictable expense. It can also mislead: a tax refund may feel like free money even though it is part of the household's resources.

Use named accounts to defend priorities, not to ignore total cost. A vacation account does not make a trip affordable if the household is carrying high-interest debt and lacks cash for next month's rent. Categories organize decisions; they do not repeal arithmetic.

Design practice: the satisfaction ledger

Review the last thirty discretionary purchases. Identify:

- five that delivered more value than expected;
- five that delivered less;
- the emotion or situation that preceded each low-value purchase;
- one category to increase deliberately;
- one category to reduce without resentment.

The goal is not minimal spending. It is a higher proportion of spending that still makes sense after the feeling that triggered it has passed.

Decision Hygiene

Clean process before confident prediction

"The fundamental law of investing is the uncertainty of the future." — ***Peter Bernstein***

Financial mistakes often begin with a sentence that contains three different things:

"The company is growing, so the stock is safe and will double in three years."

"The company is growing" may be a fact, depending on the period and measure. "The stock is safe" is a judgment. "It will double" is a forecast. When these are fused, evidence for the first claim seems to validate the other two.

Decision hygiene is the practice of keeping observations, assumptions, forecasts, and preferences separate long enough to examine them.

This is especially important because financial stories are usually coherent after the fact. A price rises and commentators locate the reason. It falls and a different reason appears. The explanation may contain truth, but coherence is not proof that the event was predictable or that the same story will forecast the next move.

The fact–estimate–story test

Divide a page into three columns.

Facts are observable and dated: the interest rate, account balance, contractual term, historical revenue, or amount due.

Estimates are uncertain quantities: future income, repair cost, market return, resale value, or probability of moving.

Stories supply meaning: *This neighborhood can only get more expensive*, *I always ruin opportunities*, or *If I wait, everyone else will get ahead.*

For a home purchase, "the payment is $2,400 under the proposed loan" is a fact about the quote. "Maintenance will average $500 a month" is an estimate. "Renting means I have failed to grow up" is a story.

All three columns matter. Stories reveal values and pressure; estimates make planning possible. The problem is letting one category impersonate another.

Use ranges and breakpoints

A single forecast creates false precision. Use a range and identify the point at which the decision changes.

Suppose a career change includes a variable bonus. Instead of budgeting the expected bonus, build the base plan on guaranteed income. Then create a rule for any bonus that actually arrives. Or, if a renovation is estimated at $40,000, ask what happens at $48,000 and $55,000. The breakpoint is the amount at which you would reduce scope, delay, borrow, or cancel.

The same method applies to investing. Do not ask only, "What return do I expect?" Ask, "What result does the goal require, what range of outcomes can the plan withstand, and which variables can I control if the return is lower?" Savings rate, goal timing, and spending flexibility may offer more reliable adjustment than a more heroic forecast.

Record disconfirming evidence

Before a major commitment, write the strongest reason not to proceed. If you cannot articulate one, you may be researching for reassurance rather than understanding.

Use four questions:

1. What would have to be true for this choice to work?
2. Which assumption is least supported?
3. What evidence would change my mind?
4. What is the cost of being wrong, not only the probability?

This is not pessimism. It is respect for consequence.

Create a source ladder

Not all information deserves equal weight. For a consequential choice, move up the ladder:

1. social posts, promotional content, anecdotes;

2. journalism and explanatory summaries;

3. product disclosures, contracts, audited statements, regulatory filings;

4. qualified professional interpretation when the material is technical or personally consequential.

Lower rungs can identify questions. They should not be the only support for answers involving taxes, legal rights, insurance coverage, or concentrated investment risk.

Design practice: the one-page brief

For your next major decision, create a one-page brief with these headings:

- Decision and deadline
- Goal served
- Facts
- Estimates and ranges
- Stories and social pressures
- Alternatives, including doing nothing for now
- Worst plausible consequence
- Reversal or exit plan
- Evidence that would change the decision
- Review date

Confidence is not the objective. A decision can remain uncertain after excellent analysis. The objective is to know which part of your conclusion rests on evidence, which part rests on a forecast, and which part expresses a value you are consciously choosing.

PART III

Build a Plan You Can Continue

Three Kinds of Risk

"How much risk can you handle?" is incomplete

"High investment rewards can be achieved only at the cost of substantial risk-taking."

— Burton G. Malkiel

Two people can choose the same investment for entirely different reasons. One has stable income, a twenty-year horizon, ample reserves, and no need to sell during a decline. The other may need the money in eighteen months and is relying on an optimistic return to close a gap. Their emotional comfort might be identical. Their capacity for loss is not.

Risk decisions become clearer when divided into three questions:

1. **Capacity:** How much loss or volatility can the plan absorb without missing essential obligations?

2. **Requirement:** How much growth does the goal reasonably need, after considering savings, time, and flexibility?

3. **Tolerance:** How much uncertainty can you live through without abandoning the plan?

FINRA similarly distinguishes willingness from capacity and notes that capacity relates to factors such as time horizon, liquidity needs, and objectives. Its investor guidance emphasizes considering objectives, needs, horizon, and tolerance together—not tolerance in isolation.

Capacity is structural

Capacity depends on the rest of your financial life. Ask:

- When will this money be needed?
- Could the date move?
- Are near-term obligations held elsewhere?

- How stable is income?
- What debts or guarantees could create a cash demand?
- Who depends on these assets?
- What would force a sale at a bad time?

Marisol and Ben both dislike market declines. Marisol is investing for retirement in twenty-five years, has six months of essential expenses in cash, and can adjust contributions during a job interruption. Ben is investing the down payment for a home he hopes to buy next year. Even if Ben feels braver, the short horizon and fixed purpose reduce his capacity for fluctuation.

Capacity can change quickly. A new child, job loss, adjustable-rate debt, divorce, illness, or planned purchase may alter it before risk tolerance feels any different.

Requirement is the neglected question

People sometimes take more risk because they want more return, not because the goal requires it. "More" has no finish line.

Translate the goal into variables:

- amount needed;
- time available;
- current assets;
- ongoing contribution;
- range of plausible returns;
- flexibility in timing or amount.

If the plan works with a moderate assumption and an affordable contribution, greater risk may be unnecessary. If the plan works only under an unusually high return, the problem may be the goal, timeline, or savings rate. Risk cannot safely repair every arithmetic gap.

Requirement also prevents excessive caution. Holding all long-term money in low-yield cash may feel safe while exposing a distant goal to inflation and insufficient growth. Safety must be defined relative to the goal, not only to short-term account stability.

Tolerance is behavior under conditions

Questionnaires can begin a conversation, but reported comfort is not the same as observed behavior. Tolerance is affected by recent experience, account size, life stress, news exposure, and whether a loss is hypothetical or visible in dollars.

Study your behavior:

- What did you do during the last decline?
- How often did you check?
- Did you change a plan or seek reassurance?
- Which dollar loss became hard to tolerate?
- Did discomfort come from volatility, uncertainty, regret, or fear of looking foolish?

Someone who claims high tolerance but repeatedly sells during declines does not need a more inspiring speech. The plan or the environment needs to change. A theoretically efficient allocation that cannot be maintained may be inferior to a more conservative allocation that survives.

Resolve conflicts among the three

The three dimensions will not always agree.

- **High capacity, low tolerance:** Reduce exposure to a maintainable level, improve understanding, limit monitoring, or add guided review.
- **Low capacity, high tolerance:** Protect the goal. Courage cannot extend a deadline or replace liquidity.
- **High requirement, low capacity:** Rework the goal, contribution, or timeline rather than pretending risk has disappeared.
- **Low requirement, high capacity:** Decide whether additional risk serves a real purpose or merely the desire to maximize.

Design practice: the risk card

For each major goal, create a card:

- Goal and target date
- Minimum acceptable outcome
- Capacity constraints
- Required range of return
- Tolerance evidence from past behavior
- Maximum allocation change allowed outside a scheduled review
- Person to contact before an exception

Risk is not a personality badge. It is a relationship among a goal, a balance sheet, a timeline, and a human nervous system.

Time Buckets and Continuity

Give time a visible place in the plan

"A budget is your Say Yes plan." — ***Tiffany Aliche***

An account statement groups money by institution. Your life uses money by date and purpose. Confusion begins when those maps are mistaken for each other.

A single brokerage account might contain next year's tuition, a future home purchase, and retirement assets. The account can look diversified while the goals are not properly separated. When markets fall, every dollar may feel equally endangered because the owner cannot see which dollars are needed soon.

Create three planning buckets—not necessarily three products, but three clearly documented jobs.

Near: money expected to support obligations and goals in roughly the next two years. Liquidity and stability dominate.

Middle: money for goals several years away, where some fluctuation may be acceptable but the date and flexibility matter.

Far: money for long-horizon goals, where short-term variation may be tolerable and growth may have time to work.

The boundaries are not universal. A person with variable income, health uncertainty, or a nonnegotiable purchase date may use a larger near bucket. The purpose is to link every dollar to a time horizon before choosing how it should be held.

Build a continuity floor

An emergency fund is often presented as a multiple of monthly expenses. That is a useful starting point, not a complete design.

Define a **continuity floor**: the minimum resources and payments needed to keep essential life functioning during disruption. Include housing, food, utilities, insurance, health needs, required debt payments, transportation, and support obligations that truly cannot pause.

Then ask what events the floor must cover:

- delayed income;

- job transition;
- major repair;
- medical deductible;
- caregiving interruption;
- relocation;
- a gap between insurance loss and reimbursement.

Separate predictable irregular expenses from emergencies. Annual premiums, car maintenance, holidays, and known travel are not surprises merely because they are not monthly. Sinking funds for these costs protect the emergency reserve from ordinary life.

Time is powerful only when participation continues

Compound-growth examples are often used as magic tricks. The useful lesson is more modest: contributions, time, and return interact, and interruption can be costly.

For illustration, $500 contributed at the end of every month for twenty years at a constant 7 percent annual return, compounded monthly, would grow to about $260,000. Contributions total $120,000; the rest is mathematical growth. Real returns are not constant, and taxes, fees, inflation, and account rules change the outcome. The example is not a forecast. It shows why a plan that can continue through ordinary stress may matter more than one optimized so tightly that the first disruption stops it.

Continuity has levels. During a difficult period, the best available action might be:

1. maintain full planned contributions;

2. reduce contributions but keep the automatic process active;

3. pause new contributions while leaving long-term assets undisturbed;

4. use the continuity reserve under a defined rule;

5. liquidate long-term assets only after reviewing taxes, penalties, alternatives, and the effect on the goal.

The levels prevent an all-or-nothing response. A temporary reduction is not the same as abandoning the system.

Do not borrow stability from the wrong horizon

Using long-term assets for a near-term need can create a chain reaction: a forced sale, tax consequence, reduced future growth, and reluctance to restart. Conversely, keeping every far-future dollar in cash to avoid fluctuation can make the long-term goal depend on increasingly large contributions.

The point of buckets is not to predict. It is to avoid asking one pool of money to be instantly stable, highly liquid, and maximally productive at the same time.

Design practice: the horizon map

List every account and every major goal. For each goal, record:

- earliest likely use date;
- latest acceptable use date;
- whether the amount is fixed or flexible;
- what happens if the value is lower when needed;
- which account currently serves it;
- whether that account also serves a conflicting horizon.

Resolve conflicts in the plan, even if you keep the same accounts. A written allocation by purpose is better than assuming the account label explains the job.

A Personal Investment Constitution

Write the rules before the argument

"It's not how much money you make. It's how much money you keep—and how hard that money works for you." — ***Robert Kiyosaki***

An investment plan often exists as a collection of intentions: stay diversified, think long term, avoid panic. These statements are agreeable and operationally weak. Under pressure, each can be reinterpreted.

A personal investment constitution is a short document that gives those intentions authority. It does not predict the future. It defines the conditions under which you will act.

Jordan believed he was a long-term investor. He also changed holdings whenever a persuasive article made his existing choices feel unsophisticated. Each trade had a reason. Together they formed no strategy. His constitution reduced the role of persuasion by requiring every proposed change to answer the same questions.

The eight sections

1. **Purpose.** State what the portfolio is for. "Grow money" is too vague. Name the goals, dates, and people served.

2. **Constraints.** Record liquidity needs, taxes, account restrictions, concentrated positions, ethical boundaries, and circumstances that could force a withdrawal.

3. **Allocation.** Define allowed asset categories and target ranges. Ranges are more useful than a single point because ordinary movement does not require constant intervention.

4. **Contributions.** State amounts or percentages, timing, and the rule for raises, bonuses, and temporary reductions.

5. **Rebalancing.** Choose a calendar, threshold, or combination. Specify whether contributions will be used first to restore targets before assets are sold.

6. Change rules. Identify what can justify a strategic change: a goal, horizon, liquidity need, tax situation, or well-supported change in assumptions. A price decline by itself is not a change in personal circumstances.

7. Decision safeguards. Include a waiting period, source requirements, and the people consulted before a large change.

8. Review. Set scheduled dates and define what data will be examined.

The constitution should be understandable by another adult in your household. Complexity that only its author can interpret is fragile.

Define sell rules carefully

"I will sell when it feels dangerous" delegates the choice to state. "I will never sell" ignores taxes, goals, rebalancing, changing circumstances, fraud, and the possibility that an investment no longer fits its assigned role.

A sell rule might include:

- the goal requires a planned distribution;
- rebalancing moves an allocation back within its range;
- the investment no longer meets written eligibility criteria;
- concentration exceeds a defined limit;
- a tax or legal change materially alters the plan;
- personal capacity or horizon has changed;
- the original thesis is contradicted by specified evidence.

For individual securities, define the thesis when buying. If you cannot state what evidence would invalidate it, the thesis may be admiration rather than analysis.

Make exceptions expensive in thought, not money

Every constitution needs an amendment process. Otherwise a genuine life change can make the rules harmful. But amendment should require more than an urgent feeling.

Use an exception form:

- rule being changed;

- new circumstance;
- evidence;
- alternatives considered;
- immediate and long-term cost;
- cooling-off period;
- date the new rule will be reviewed.

The form creates intellectual friction. It also reveals repeated exceptions, which usually mean the written rule is unrealistic or the same cue keeps overruling it.

Household governance

In a shared financial life, decide who can do what. One partner may handle execution while both approve strategic changes. Set thresholds for unilateral spending, lending, account openings, and changes in risk. Record where documents and credentials are stored, how bills will be paid if one person is unavailable, and who can communicate with professionals.

Governance is not distrust. It prevents ordinary asymmetry in attention or expertise from becoming invisible control.

Design practice: draft the constitution

Limit the first draft to two pages. Use plain language. If a section is unknown, mark it "to be decided" and schedule the decision. Sign and date the document, even if only for yourself.

Then test it against three scenarios:

- markets fall sharply;

- income stops for six months;

- an attractive new investment dominates conversation among people you respect.

If the document does not tell you what to do next—or at least what not to do yet—it is still a statement of values, not an operating plan.

PART IV

Stay Adaptive

Information Boundaries

Information has a behavioral cost

"Don't try to buy at the bottom and sell at the top. This can't be done—except by liars." — ***Bernard Baruch***

Financial information is usually treated as an unqualified good. More data should produce better decisions. But information also changes attention, emotion, and the perceived need to act.

Research across seventeen countries found that, on average, people showed stronger physiological activation to negative television news than to positive news, with meaningful individual variation (Soroka et al., 2019). Financial media operate in the same attention economy. Sudden losses, conflict, prediction, and danger are naturally compelling. A headline can be accurate and still be irrelevant to your next action.

Noah checked market news throughout the workday. He considered himself informed, yet could not identify a single planned decision the checking improved. It made ordinary volatility feel like a series of emergencies and filled his mind with assets he did not own. His information habit created decisions rather than supporting them.

Use the actionability test

Before consuming an update, ask:

1. Which decision could this information change?
2. Am I authorized and prepared to make that decision now?
3. What source would be sufficient?
4. When is the next scheduled review?

If there is no decision, the information may be education, entertainment, or emotional monitoring. Name it honestly. Entertainment is allowed; it should not be confused with fiduciary work on your own behalf.

Information is actionable when it affects a rule or assumption tied to your life: an interest rate on debt you can refinance, a benefit-election deadline, a tax notice, a change in insurance coverage, or a goal whose funding has materially shifted. A commentator's year-end market target rarely changes a long-term household obligation.

Match frequency to the horizon

The frequency of observation can transform the apparent character of an asset. A long-horizon investment viewed minute by minute becomes an emotional object. A variable that is acceptable over years can feel intolerable when every decline is made salient.

Set a monitoring schedule by job:

- transaction accounts: often enough to detect fraud and manage cash flow;
- bills and debt: aligned with due dates and rate changes;
- goal progress: monthly or quarterly, depending on the goal;
- long-term allocation: on the schedule in the investment constitution;
- breaking financial news: only when it affects an identified decision or obligation.

Alerts should point to action. A fraud alert has a clear response. A generic "your portfolio moved" alert may only create arousal.

Build a source hierarchy

Choose sources before a crisis. For each area, name the primary source:

- employer or plan administrator for benefit rules;
- insurer and policy document for coverage;
- tax authority and qualified tax professional for tax obligations;

- regulator, filing, prospectus, and qualified adviser for investment details;

- lender and signed agreement for loan terms.

Commentary can help you understand those sources. It should not overwrite them.

Be particularly cautious with content that combines urgency, certainty, identity, and a transaction. “Smart investors are moving now” is not evidence. It is a social instruction attached to a sales cue.

Create a response ladder

When alarming information arrives, use three stages.

Observe: What exactly happened? Record the source and date.

Relevance: Which goal, account, obligation, or assumption does it affect?

Response: What does the written plan require, and is action due now?

Most headlines will stop at relevance. That is not negligence. It is filtering.

Design practice: the financial media diet

For two weeks:

- remove price alerts that have no defined response;

- schedule one period for financial news rather than checking continuously;

- keep a list of headlines that made you want to act;

- record whether they changed any fact in your plan;

- unsubscribe from one source that repeatedly produces urgency without useful decisions.

At the end, measure not only what you learned but what the information made you do. A media diet is successful when it improves decision quality, not when it maximizes exposure.

Transition Mode

A plan needs a lower gear

"People first. Then money. Then things." — ***Suze Orman***

Most plans describe normal operations. Life also contains layoffs, illness, caregiving, separation, relocation, business interruption, and grief. These events reduce attention at the same time they increase financial complexity.

Without a transition protocol, people often choose between two extremes: pretend nothing has changed or dismantle the whole plan. A lower gear creates a third option.

Transition mode is a temporary operating state with three goals:

1. protect essentials;
2. preserve as much continuity as circumstances allow;
3. defer decisions that do not need to be made under pressure.

It is not failure. It is part of the design.

Define the trigger

Transition mode should begin when a specified event occurs, not when guilt finally permits it. Possible triggers include:

- income falls below a set percentage of normal;
- essential expenses rise beyond a threshold;
- a household member cannot perform their usual financial role;
- a separation, death, move, or caregiving event changes obligations;
- available reserves fall below a defined level;
- cognitive or emotional load makes ordinary review unsafe.

Write the trigger while life is stable. In disruption, interpretation is expensive.

Use a transition ledger

Create a single document with four sections.

Cash now: balances, income expected, essential expenses, minimum debt payments, insurance deductibles, and benefits available.

Decisions due: deadlines that cannot move, such as coverage elections, tax filings, housing notices, or required distributions.

Decisions deferred: renovations, discretionary investing changes, major gifts, new long-term commitments, or anything primarily intended to restore a sense of normality.

People and permissions: professionals, family members, account access, powers of attorney, and who is responsible for each next action.

The ledger prevents every concern from occupying the same mental priority.

Step down deliberately

Define levels of reduction before liquidation.

Level 1: trim. Pause optional purchases and redirect discretionary cash flow.

Level 2: reduce. Lower contributions or extra debt payments temporarily while protecting required payments and coverage.

Level 3: use reserves. Draw from the funds built for disruption under the rules established in the horizon map.

Level 4: restructure. Renegotiate obligations, change housing or transportation, or revise goals with professional input where needed.

Level 5: liquidate long-term assets. Review taxes, penalties, sequence, concentration, and the cost to future goals before acting.

Real emergencies may skip levels. The ladder is not meant to delay necessary care or safety. It prevents an uncomfortable but manageable month from being treated as a permanent collapse.

Put a date on temporary choices

A pause without a restart condition quietly becomes a new default. Every transition decision needs a review date.

For example:

Retirement contributions will fall from 10 percent to 3 percent for three pay periods. On October 15, we will review income and reserves. If income has recovered above the stated threshold, contributions return automatically to 7 percent, then increase by one point per month until the prior level is restored.

The exact numbers are personal. The structure matters: amount, duration, threshold, and next step.

Protect the bereaved and overwhelmed self

After a death, diagnosis, separation, or job loss, people are often pressured to make large financial decisions quickly. Some deadlines are real. Many are not.

Use the sentence: "What is the actual deadline, and where is it documented?" Ask which choices are reversible. Keep proceeds from a sale or insurance payment in a secure, understandable place while a longer-term plan is developed. Be skeptical of anyone who converts grief into urgency for a product.

Transition mode may require legal, tax, insurance, or mental-health support. Asking for expertise is not surrendering control; it is assigning a task to the right layer of the system.

Design practice: the one-page transition protocol

Write:

- the events that activate transition mode;
- essential monthly costs;
- the location and purpose of reserves;
- the sequence of reductions;
- actions prohibited without a second review;
- the people who can help;
- the first review date;
- the conditions for returning to normal operation.

You cannot make disruption convenient. You can keep it from erasing every decision made before it arrived.

The Review System

A plan becomes trustworthy through maintenance

"A budget is telling your money where to go, instead of wondering where it went."
—John C. Maxwell

Financial plans fail quietly. A subscription renews. A beneficiary remains outdated. A raise is absorbed. An allocation drifts. An emergency transfer becomes a new level of spending. Nothing feels large enough to demand attention, so the system changes without being redesigned.

Review is how a plan learns.

Monitoring goal progress generally improves attainment, particularly when progress is recorded or made public in an appropriate setting (Harkin et al., 2016). In financial life, monitoring must be structured carefully: too little allows drift, while constant observation can provoke needless action. The solution is a cadence matched to the type of decision.

The monthly maintenance meeting

Set a recurring thirty-minute appointment. If money is shared, include the people who share responsibility. Use the same agenda:

1. **Cash flow:** Did income, essential spending, debt, or transfers differ materially from the plan?

2. **Exceptions:** Which rules were overridden, and why?

3. **Upcoming irregular costs:** What is due in the next ninety days?

4. **Protection:** Any fraud, coverage, beneficiary, document, or access issue?

5. **One adjustment:** What single change would make next month easier?

Do not turn the meeting into a forensic reconstruction of every coffee. Investigate patterns that affect goals, create conflict, or reveal a broken process.

The quarterly calibration

Once a quarter, zoom out:

- progress toward each goal;
- savings and debt trends;
- account roles and time horizons;
- allocation versus policy ranges;
- risk capacity changes;
- recurring low-value spending;
- unresolved financial decisions;
- status of transition-mode reductions or pauses.

The question is not "Did the market go up?" It is "Did the household do what the plan assigned, and does the assignment still fit?"

Use traffic-light labels:

- **Green:** on course; no change needed.
- **Amber:** watch a threshold or correct a small drift.
- **Red:** a goal, obligation, or capacity constraint requires a decision.

Labels compress complexity without pretending precision.

The annual redesign

Annual review is for structure, not merely balances. Ask:

- Which goals are complete, new, or no longer important?

- What changed in family, health, work, location, or responsibility?

- Are insurance and estate documents aligned with current life?

- Has tax status changed?

- Does the investment constitution still fit capacity, requirement, and tolerance?

- Which default produced the most value?

- Which source of friction repeatedly failed?

- What did the decision records reveal about cues and states?

Update rules openly. A changed rule is not evidence that the original plan was useless. It is evidence that the review system is functioning.

Measure process as well as outcomes

Net worth, debt, and savings matter. They are not fully controllable over short periods. Add process measures:

- percentage of planned transfers completed;
- number of unscheduled investment changes;
- count of high-stakes decisions made in amber or red;
- number of exceptions without a review date;
- days of essential expenses available;
- percentage of important accounts with current beneficiaries;
- frequency of money conversations completed as scheduled.

Process measures identify improvement before outcomes become dramatic. They also prevent a favorable market from disguising bad behavior or an unfavorable market from making a sound process look foolish.

Review without prosecution

Shame reduces the quality of information. If every review becomes a trial, people hide transactions, avoid statements, and defend choices they might otherwise examine.

Use neutral language:

- "The transfer was canceled after the car repair" instead of "We failed again."

- "Three purchases followed conflict at work" instead of "I am irresponsible."

- "The rule produced repeated exceptions" instead of "I have no discipline."

Neutral does not mean permissive. Consequences remain real. The point is to describe the mechanism accurately enough to change it.

Design practice: schedule the system

Before closing this chapter, place three events on the calendar:

- monthly maintenance;
- quarterly calibration;
- annual redesign.

Attach the agenda to each event. Assign an owner. Decide where decisions and amendments will be stored.

A review that depends on remembering is not yet part of the system.

Conclusion: A System You Can Trust

"You can afford anything, but not everything." — ***Paula Pant***

Financial confidence is often described as certainty: knowing the correct answer, choosing the right investment, or feeling untroubled by risk. That kind of confidence is fragile because the future can always produce a question you have not studied and an event you did not predict.

A more durable confidence comes from process.

You know how to recognize a decision loop before it completes itself. You can distinguish a signal from the state and story wrapped around it. You can identify an inherited money rule and rewrite it as a policy. You can use defaults to make chosen behavior ordinary and friction to slow choices that deserve scrutiny. You can test spending by the value it actually creates.

You can separate facts, estimates, and narratives. You can examine capacity, requirement, and tolerance instead of treating risk as a measure of bravery. You can give money a job and a horizon, protect a continuity floor, and write investment rules before the next argument begins. You can limit information that creates action without relevance. You can shift into transition mode without declaring the plan dead. And you can review the system on a schedule that allows it to learn.

None of this removes uncertainty. It changes your relationship to it.

Return to the sentence you wrote in the introduction: *The money behavior I most want to understand is...*

Now answer five questions:

1. What signal usually begins it?
2. Which state gives the signal authority?
3. What story makes the behavior feel necessary?
4. Which feature of the environment makes it easy?
5. What review would reveal whether the change is working?

Choose one intervention. Not twelve. Add a pause rule, automate a transfer, remove stored payment details, define a family-support limit, write a sell rule, or schedule the monthly review.

Then observe what happens.

The aim is not to become a flawless financial machine. It is to build a humane system—one that expects emotion, allows recovery, protects what matters, and makes your considered decisions easier to keep.

That is what it means to put money by design.

Appendix: The Money by Design Toolkit

The tools below collect the book's practices in reusable form. Print them, place them in a shared digital document, or adapt them to the system you already use. A tool is valuable only if it appears at the moment of decision.

Tool 1: Decision Record

Decision:

Date and actual deadline:

Amount or consequence:

Signal

What happened immediately before I wanted to act?

State

Green, amber, or red? What do I notice physically and emotionally?

Story

What sentence makes action feel necessary? Which part is identity, prediction, or social pressure?

Facts

What is observed, documented, and dated?

Estimates

What ranges am I using? Which estimate is least supported?

Options

What are the next-best alternative, a smaller version, and the option to wait?

Protection

What makes this reversible? What is the cost of being wrong?

Review

What did I expect to happen, by when, and when will I examine the result?

Tool 2: If–Then Plan Builder

Use one observable cue and one specific response.

If __________ *happens, then I will* __________ *before I* __________.

Examples:

- If I want to change a long-term investment after reading news, then I will close the app and review my constitution the next morning before placing an order.

- If a family request exceeds the balance in the support account, then I will wait forty-eight hours and discuss the request with my partner before agreeing.

- If a discretionary purchase exceeds my threshold, then I will record it on the waiting list before checking out.

Test the plan: Can another person tell whether the cue occurred? Is the response possible in that moment? Does it include a time or place? Does it protect the goal rather than merely delay discomfort?

Tool 3: Monthly Maintenance Agenda

Date:

People present:
Time limit: 30 minutes

1. Did income or essential spending change materially?

2. Were planned bills, transfers, and debt payments completed?

3. Which exceptions occurred? What cue and state preceded them?

4. Which irregular expenses are due in the next ninety days?

5. Are there fraud, coverage, beneficiary, document, or account-access issues?

6. Is transition mode active, or should it be activated?

7. What single adjustment will make the next month easier?

Owner of adjustment:

Completion date:

End the meeting when the agenda is complete. Add technical questions to a separate list rather than allowing research to consume the review.

Tool 4: Goal and Horizon Card

Goal:

Person or purpose served:

Target amount or range:

Earliest use date:

Latest acceptable use date:

Current assets assigned:

Ongoing contribution:

Capacity

What loss, delay, or variation can the plan absorb? What would force a sale?

Requirement

What return range does the goal need under current contributions? What can change if the range is lower?

Tolerance

How have I actually behaved during uncertainty? Which dollar or percentage decline became difficult?

Continuity

Which near-term resources keep this goal from being raided during disruption?

Review date:

Tool 5: Two-Page Investment Constitution

Purpose

List every goal the portfolio serves and the approximate horizon for each.

Constraints

List liquidity, tax, legal, concentration, ethical, income, and household constraints.

Allowed investments and allocation ranges

Use language you understand. If an asset cannot be explained, it is not yet eligible.

Contribution rule

State amount or percentage, timing, and the rule for raises and bonuses.

Rebalancing rule

State the calendar or threshold and the order of operations.

Change and sell rules

List the changes in goals, capacity, assumptions, or evidence that can justify action.

Safeguards

State waiting periods, approval thresholds, required sources, and people consulted.

Review and amendment

State review dates and the form required for exceptions.

Signed:

Date:

Tool 6: Transition Protocol

Activation events

List income, health, family, or reserve conditions that move the household into transition mode.

Continuity floor

Record one month of essential costs and the reserves assigned to them.

Reduction sequence

1. Optional spending to trim
2. Contributions or extra payments that may be reduced
3. Reserves and the order in which they may be used
4. Obligations that could be restructured
5. Long-term assets and required professional review before liquidation

Protected actions

List bills, coverage, care, and deadlines that continue.

Prohibited actions

List new commitments, gifts, purchases, or investment changes that require a second review.

Decision bench

Name the technical expert, grounded confidant, and affected household member.

First review date:

Condition for returning to normal operation:

Tool 7: Annual Redesign Scorecard

Rate each category green, amber, or red:

- cash-flow reliability;
- high-interest debt;
- continuity reserves;
- insurance and essential protections;
- beneficiary and estate-document alignment;
- goal funding;
- allocation within policy ranges;
- risk capacity and tolerance fit;
- recurring spending satisfaction;
- household communication;
- financial document access;
- quality of information sources;
- number and pattern of rule exceptions.

For every amber or red item, choose one of four actions: repair now, schedule, seek expertise, or consciously accept. “Worry about it” is not an action category.

Bonus Section

Every book should have a bonus section with freebies!

First, there are a few more of my favorite financial quotes I'd like to share:

"The four most dangerous words in investing are: 'This time it's different.'"

— Sir John Templeton

"We simply attempt to be fearful when others are greedy and to be greedy only when others are fearful." — ***Warren Buffett***

"Our favorite holding period is forever." — ***Warren Buffett***

"The first rule of compounding is to never interrupt it unnecessarily." — ***Charlie Munger***

"The biggest risk of all is not taking one." — ***Mellody Hobson***

"Invest in what you know." — ***Peter Lynch***

"Never spend your money before you have it." — ***Thomas Jefferson***

BOGO Time! You bought one book but get a second one free!

Free access to my latest research report:

WHEN MARKETS STOP CLOSING: Tokenized Equities, 24/7 Stock Trading, and Dinari's Bid to Put U.S. Shares Onchain

https://bit.ly/4fNiy3H

Visit my books website:

https://brucehoyt.com/

Financial Terms and Key Concepts

This plain-language glossary explains the financial terms used in the book and adds several closely related terms that readers may encounter when applying its ideas. Definitions are educational, not individualized financial, investment, tax, legal, or insurance advice. Product terms and laws can change

0-9

401(k) plan: An employer-sponsored retirement plan that lets eligible employees contribute part of their pay. Contributions may be pre-tax or Roth, if the plan offers both choices, and employers may provide matching contributions. Tax rules, limits, and withdrawal restrictions apply.

A

Account balance: The amount shown in an account at a particular time. An investment account balance changes with contributions, withdrawals, fees, and market value; it is not a guarantee of what the account will be worth later.

Account statement: A periodic record of account activity, including balances, deposits, withdrawals, purchases, sales, interest, dividends, and fees. Statements should be reviewed for accuracy, fraud, and changes that affect the plan.

Adjustable-rate debt: Debt whose interest rate can change according to the loan agreement, often after an introductory period or when a reference rate moves. A higher rate can increase the payment and total borrowing cost.

Allocation; asset allocation: The way investment money is divided among asset classes such as stocks, bonds, and cash. A suitable allocation depends on the investor's goals, time horizon, liquidity needs, risk capacity, and risk tolerance.

Annual percentage rate (APR): A standardized annual measure of borrowing cost that generally includes the interest rate and certain fees. APR helps compare credit offers, although variable rates, promotional periods, and excluded charges still require review.

Asset: Anything with economic value that a person or household owns or controls, such as cash, a home, a vehicle, retirement savings, or investments. Assets are one side of a personal balance sheet.

Asset class or category: A broad group of investments with similar characteristics, such as stocks, bonds, cash equivalents, or real estate. Different classes may respond differently to economic and market conditions.

Audited financial statements: Company financial reports examined by an independent auditor for conformity with applicable accounting standards. An audit adds assurance but does not guarantee future performance or eliminate fraud and investment risk.

Automatic enrollment: A plan feature that enrolls an eligible person unless that person opts out. In a workplace retirement plan, the default contribution rate and investment choice may remain in place until the participant changes them.

Automatic transfer: A recurring electronic movement of money between accounts on a preset schedule. It can support saving or bill payment, but the amount and timing should be monitored to avoid shortfalls or overdrafts.

B

Balance sheet: A snapshot of assets and liabilities at a specific date. For a household, subtracting total liabilities from total assets produces net worth.

Beneficiary: A person, trust, estate, charity, or other entity designated to receive money or property from an account, insurance policy, retirement plan, or estate arrangement. Designations should be reviewed after major life changes.

Bond: A debt security through which an investor lends money to a government, company, or other issuer. The issuer generally promises interest and repayment of principal, but credit, interest-rate, inflation, and market risks remain.

Brokerage account: An account held with a brokerage firm for buying, holding, and selling investments. A standard brokerage account is generally taxable; retirement brokerage accounts follow the tax rules of the retirement arrangement.

Budget: A plan for directing income among spending, saving, debt repayment, and other priorities over a defined period. A useful budget reflects both essential obligations and deliberate choices rather than serving only as a restriction.

Buy now, pay later (BNPL): A short-term installment arrangement that divides a purchase into multiple payments. Some plans charge no interest, but late fees, automatic withdrawals, missed-payment consequences, and credit reporting practices can vary.

C

Capital gain or capital loss: The difference between an asset's sale proceeds and its adjusted cost basis. A gain or loss may have tax consequences that depend on the asset, account type, holding period, and current tax law.

Cash and cash equivalents: Cash plus highly liquid, short-term holdings that can generally be converted to cash with limited price fluctuation. Examples may include insured deposits and certain short-term instruments; investment products are not automatically FDIC-insured.

Cash flow: Money entering and leaving a household during a period. Positive cash flow means inflows exceed outflows; negative cash flow means spending, transfers, and payments exceed incoming money.

Collateral: Property or another asset pledged to secure a loan. If the borrower does not meet the agreement, the lender may have the right to take or sell the collateral, subject to the contract and law.

Compound interest or compound growth: Growth produced when earnings remain invested and can generate additional earnings. Compounding can accelerate growth over time, but actual investment returns vary and may be reduced by taxes, fees, inflation, and losses.

Concentrated position: A large share of a portfolio held in one company, security, industry, or closely related group. Concentration can magnify gains, losses, and liquidity problems and may reduce the benefits of diversification.

Consumer debt: Money borrowed for personal or household purchases rather than business investment. Examples include credit-card balances, personal loans, auto loans, and some installment plans; rates, collateral, and repayment terms differ.

Continuity floor: The book's term for the minimum resources needed to keep essential life functioning during disruption. It includes core expenses, required payments, coverage, and reserves matched to realistic interruption risks.

Contribution: Money added to a savings, investment, or retirement account. Contributions may be one-time or recurring and may be subject to plan eligibility, tax treatment, annual limits, employer matching rules, and withdrawal restrictions.

Cost basis: Generally, the amount invested in an asset, adjusted for items such as reinvested distributions, certain fees, improvements, splits, or prior tax events. Cost basis helps determine taxable gain or loss when an asset is sold.

Credit card: A revolving credit account that permits purchases or cash advances up to an approved limit. Interest may be avoided on eligible purchases by paying the statement balance on time, but terms, fees, and grace periods vary.

Credit score: A number calculated from information in a credit report to estimate credit risk. Lenders may use different scoring models, and a score can influence approval, interest rates, limits, deposits, and other credit terms.

D

Debt: Money or another obligation owed to a lender or creditor under agreed terms. Important features include principal, interest rate, payment schedule, repayment deadline, fees, collateral, and consequences of missed payments.

Debt-to-income ratio (DTI): Monthly debt obligations divided by gross monthly income, expressed as a percentage. Lenders often use DTI when evaluating repayment capacity, but the calculation method and acceptable range vary by lender and product.

Deductible: The amount a policyholder generally must pay toward a covered loss or service before an insurer pays according to the policy. Deductibles and exceptions differ by insurance type and contract.

Default: In this book, a default often means the option or action that occurs automatically when no new choice is made. In lending, default separately means failure to meet a debt obligation under the contract.

Discretionary spending: Spending that is not required for immediate essential obligations and can usually be reduced, delayed, or changed. What is discretionary depends on the household's circumstances, responsibilities, and values.

Diversification: Spreading investments among different assets and exposures so one holding or risk does not dominate the portfolio. Diversification can reduce certain risks but cannot guarantee a profit or prevent every loss.

Dividend: A payment a corporation or fund may make to shareholders from earnings, income, or other available resources. Dividends are not guaranteed and may be reduced, suspended, reinvested, or taxable.

E

Emergency fund or emergency reserve: Money set aside for genuine disruptions such as income loss, urgent repairs, or unexpected health costs. The appropriate size and location depend on essential expenses, income stability, insurance, access needs, and household risks.

Employer match: Money an employer contributes to an employee's retirement account under the plan's formula, often based on the employee's own contributions. Eligibility, ownership rules, limits, and matching formulas vary by plan.

Estate documents: Legal documents that direct financial and personal matters during incapacity or after death. They may include a will, trust, beneficiary designations, powers of attorney, and health-care directives; state law and personal circumstances matter.

Exchange-traded fund (ETF): A pooled investment product whose shares trade on a securities exchange. ETFs can hold stocks, bonds, or other assets; their risks, objectives, prices, fees, tax effects, and trading characteristics vary.

Expense ratio and investment fees: An expense ratio is a fund's annual operating expenses expressed as a percentage of average net assets. Trading costs, advisory fees, sales charges, and account fees may be separate and can materially reduce long-term results.

F

FDIC deposit insurance: Federal insurance for eligible deposit accounts at insured banks, subject to coverage categories, ownership rules, and limits. It does not insure stocks, bonds, mutual funds, crypto assets, or the market value of investments.

Fiduciary: A person or organization required in a particular relationship to act in another party's best interest. The exact duty and scope depend on the law, role, service, and agreement; the title 'financial professional' alone does not define the duty.

Financial adviser or financial planner: A broad label for professionals who may provide investment, planning, insurance, tax-related, or other financial services. Credentials, registration, compensation, duties, and permitted services differ, so qualifications and conflicts should be verified.

Fixed-rate debt: Debt with an interest rate that remains fixed for the period stated in the agreement. Payments may be more predictable, although taxes, insurance, fees, or other components can still change.

Forced sale: A sale made because cash is needed, a deadline arrives, collateral requirements change, or another constraint leaves little choice. Forced sales can lock in losses and may create taxes, penalties, or damage to a long-term goal.

H

High-interest debt: Debt carrying a comparatively costly interest rate, often including revolving credit-card balances and some unsecured loans. Because the balance can grow quickly, repayment may offer a reliable reduction in future interest expense.

I

Index fund: A mutual fund or ETF that seeks to track the performance of a specified market index before fees. Index funds can provide broad exposure, but they still carry market, tracking, concentration, and product-specific risks.

Inflation: A broad rise in prices that reduces the purchasing power of money over time. Inflation can make a stable account balance less useful in real terms and can affect interest rates, spending needs, and investment results.

Inheritance: Money, investments, property, or other assets received from a deceased person's estate, trust, account, or beneficiary arrangement. Taxes, debts, transfer procedures, deadlines, and planning choices may require professional guidance.

Insurance coverage: The protection an insurance policy provides for specified losses, people, property, or events, subject to exclusions, limits, deductibles, premiums, waiting periods, and claim procedures stated in the contract.

Interest: The price paid for borrowing money or the amount earned for allowing money to be used. It may be simple or compound and may be calculated differently depending on the loan, deposit, or investment.

Interest rate: The percentage used to calculate interest on borrowed or saved money over a stated period. A quoted rate should be read with the compounding method, fees, fixed or variable status, and other contract terms.

Investment constitution: The book's term for a written personal investment policy. It states the portfolio's purpose, constraints, allowed investments, target ranges, contribution and rebalancing rules, safeguards, sell rules, and review process.

Individual retirement account (IRA): A tax-advantaged retirement arrangement established by an individual. Traditional and Roth IRAs have different tax treatment, eligibility rules, contribution limits, and withdrawal rules, which can change over time.

L

Liability: A financial obligation or amount owed, such as a loan, credit-card balance, tax due, or unpaid bill. Liabilities are subtracted from assets when calculating net worth.

Lifestyle inflation: An increase in recurring spending as income rises. Some improvement in living standard may be intentional, but automatic expansion can absorb raises and reduce the amount available for saving, debt reduction, and goals.

Liquidity: How quickly and reliably an asset can be converted to spendable cash without a major loss in value or excessive cost. Liquidity needs are especially important for near-term obligations and emergency reserves.

Loan term: The period and contractual conditions under which a loan is repaid. A longer term may reduce the scheduled payment while increasing total interest, depending on the rate, fees, and repayment structure.

M

Market volatility: The degree and speed of price movement in a market or investment. Volatility can create gains or losses and may matter differently depending on the investor's horizon, liquidity needs, allocation, and behavior.

Mental accounting: The tendency to treat money differently according to its source, label, or intended purpose. Separate categories can protect priorities, but labels can also hide the household's total cost, risk, or available resources.

Minimum payment: The smallest payment a creditor requires by the due date to keep an account current under its terms. Paying only the minimum can substantially extend repayment and increase total interest.

Mutual fund: A pooled investment company that sells shares to investors and invests the proceeds according to a stated objective. Funds differ in holdings, strategy, risk, fees, tax treatment, and how shares are bought and redeemed.

N

Near, middle, and far time buckets: The book's planning categories for money needed soon, several years from now, or over a long horizon. The buckets describe purpose and timing, not necessarily separate financial products or accounts.

Net worth: Total assets minus total liabilities at a specific date. Net worth is a useful financial snapshot, but it does not by itself measure cash-flow stability, liquidity, insurance protection, or progress toward every goal.

O

Overdraft: A transaction that exceeds the available balance in a bank or credit-union account. The institution may decline the transaction, cover it, transfer funds, or charge fees according to the account agreement and applicable rules.

P

Penalty: An added financial or tax cost triggered by an action such as late payment, early withdrawal, contract cancellation, or failure to meet a rule. A penalty is separate from ordinary interest, taxes, or investment loss.

Portfolio: The complete collection of investments held by a person, household, account, or institution. Portfolio analysis considers how the holdings work together, not only whether each individual holding appears attractive.

Power of attorney: A legal document authorizing an agent to act for another person within stated powers. Financial institutions and state laws may impose requirements, so the document should be prepared and reviewed appropriately.

Premium: The amount paid for insurance coverage, usually on a recurring schedule. Paying a premium does not mean every loss is covered; deductibles, exclusions, limits, and policy conditions still apply.

Principal: The original amount borrowed, deposited, or invested, excluding interest or later earnings. Loan payments may be divided between principal, interest, and fees.

Prospectus: A required disclosure document describing an investment offering or fund, including objectives, strategies, risks, costs, management, and other material information. It should be read together with current reports and other relevant filings.

R

Rate of return: The gain or loss on an investment over a period, usually expressed as a percentage of the amount invested. Returns may be stated before or after fees, taxes, and inflation, so the measurement basis matters.

Rebalancing: Returning a portfolio toward its chosen asset-allocation targets after market movement or cash flows cause drift. Rebalancing may use new contributions, purchases, or sales and can create costs or tax consequences.

Refinancing: Replacing an existing loan with a new loan, often to change the rate, payment, term, or borrower. Closing costs, fees, a longer repayment period, and lost protections can offset a lower payment.

Regulatory filing: A document submitted to a government regulator, often containing financial, ownership, risk, or event information. Filings are primary sources, but they still require careful reading and may not answer every personal decision question.

Required minimum distribution (RMD): The minimum amount that must generally be withdrawn each year from certain retirement accounts after the applicable starting point. RMD rules differ by account and beneficiary status and can change, so current IRS guidance should be checked.

Retirement account or retirement plan: An arrangement intended for retirement saving that may receive special tax treatment. Examples include 401(k) plans and IRAs. Contribution, investment, vesting, withdrawal, distribution, and tax rules vary by arrangement.

Risk capacity: The financial ability to withstand loss or volatility without jeopardizing essential obligations or the goal. It depends on factors such as time horizon, liquidity needs, income stability, reserves, debts, flexibility, and dependents.

Risk requirement: The book's term for the amount of investment growth a goal reasonably needs after considering current assets, future contributions, time available, and flexibility. A high required return may signal that the goal, timeline, or savings rate needs revision.

Risk tolerance: The degree of uncertainty and market fluctuation an investor is willing and behaviorally able to endure. Tolerance should be considered with objectives, time horizon, liquidity needs, and risk capacity rather than used by itself.

Roth IRA: An IRA funded with after-tax contributions. Qualified distributions can be tax-free, and the original owner generally has no lifetime RMDs, but eligibility, contribution limits, holding periods, and withdrawal rules apply.

S

Savings rate: The share of income directed to savings and investment during a period. The calculation should specify whether it uses gross or take-home income and whether employer contributions are included.

Security: A tradable financial interest or instrument, such as a stock, bond, or fund share. Securities differ in ownership rights, payment promises, liquidity, regulation, and risk.

Sinking fund: Money accumulated gradually for a known but irregular future expense, such as an annual premium, vehicle repair, holiday spending, or planned travel. It keeps predictable costs from consuming emergency reserves.

Stock: A security representing an ownership interest in a corporation. Stockholders may benefit from price appreciation or dividends, but prices fluctuate and investors can lose some or all of the amount invested.

T

Take-home pay: The amount of a paycheck remaining after taxes, benefit costs, retirement contributions, and other deductions are withheld. It is the money actually deposited or paid to the worker.

Tax consequence: Any change in taxes caused by a transaction, account choice, distribution, sale, gift, or other event. Consequences may include taxable income, gains, losses, deductions, credits, withholding, or penalties and depend on current law and personal facts.

Tax-deferred or tax-advantaged account: An account receiving special tax treatment. Tax-deferred generally means tax is postponed until a later event; tax-advantaged is broader and may include deductions, deferral, tax-free qualified withdrawals, or other benefits.

Tax refund: Money returned when taxes paid or withheld exceed the final tax liability, after credits and other adjustments. A refund is generally a return of excess payment, not automatically extra income.

Target-date fund: A diversified mutual fund or ETF that generally shifts to a more conservative allocation as a stated target year approaches. Funds with the same year can differ in strategy, risk, fees, holdings, and whether the glide path continues after the date.

Time horizon: The length of time before money is expected to be used or a goal must be funded. A longer horizon can allow more recovery time, but it does not remove market, inflation, or personal risks.

Transaction account: An account designed for frequent deposits, withdrawals, payments, and transfers, such as a checking account. Its primary job is cash management rather than long-term investment growth.

Transition mode: The book's term for a temporary lower-gear financial operating state during disruption. It protects essentials, preserves feasible continuity, delays unnecessary commitments, and assigns explicit review and restart conditions.

V

Variable income: Income that changes in amount or timing, such as commissions, bonuses, tips, seasonal work, contract earnings, or business revenue. Planning often requires a conservative base, larger reserves, and rules for unusually high or low months.

W

Withdrawal or distribution: Money removed from an account. A withdrawal may reduce future growth and may trigger taxes, penalties, selling costs, or plan restrictions depending on the account, investment, age, purpose, and current rules.

Reference basis: Definitions were checked against public guidance from the SEC, CFPB, FINRA, IRS, and FDIC.

Selected References

"The investor's chief problem—and even his worst enemy—is likely to be himself."
— Benjamin Graham

https://www.ifa.com/quotes/benjamin_graham

"The future is inherently uncertain and financial markets are inherently unpredictable." — **George Soros**

https://www.georgesoros.com/2014/01/13/fallibility-reflexivity-and-the-human-uncertainty-principle-2/

"Far more money has been lost by investors preparing for corrections, or trying to anticipate corrections, than has been lost in corrections themselves." — **Peter Lynch**

https://www.fidelity.com/bin-public/060_www_fidelity_com/documents/learning-center/Fine-tuning%20your%20portfolio_Session%202_012120.pdf

"Investing should be more like watching paint dry or watching grass grow. If you want excitement, take $800 and go to Las Vegas." — **Paul Samuelson**

https://www.brainyquote.com/quotes/paul_samuelson_205549

A budget didn't limit my freedom. It actually gave me freedom!" — **Rachel Cruze**

https://www.ramseysolutions.com/rachel-cruze

"Don't look for the needle in the haystack. Just buy the haystack." — **John C. Bogle**

https://www.sec.gov/newsroom/speeches-statements/gensler-etam-051624

"The key to dealing with the future lies in knowing where you are, even if you can't know precisely where you're going." — **Howard Marks**

https://www.oaktreecapital.com/docs/default-source/memos/2001-11-20-you-cant-predict-you-can-prepare.pdf

"The fundamental law of investing is the uncertainty of the future." — **Peter Bernstein** https://equity-compass-ui.prod.csa.stifel.com/content/Insights/content/cripps_why_forecasts_matter_in_retirement_oct2023.pdf

"High investment rewards can be achieved only at the cost of substantial risk-taking." — **Burton G. Malkiel**

https://acquirersmultiple.com/2021/11/burton-malkiel-risk-tolerance-whats-your-sleeping-point/

"A budget is your Say Yes plan." — **Tiffany Aliche**

https://sobrief.com/books/get-good-with-money

"It's not how much money you make. It's how much money you keep—and how hard that money works for you." — **Robert Kiyosaki**

https://finance.yahoo.com/news/robert-kiyosaki-learn-rich-000012722.html

"Don't try to buy at the bottom and sell at the top. This can't be done—except by liars." — **Bernard Baruch**

https://novelinvestor.com/notes/baruch-my-own-story/

"People first. Then money. Then things." — **Suze Orman**

https://www.suzeorman.com/blog/people-first-this-holiday-season/

"A budget is telling your money where to go, instead of wondering where it went." — **John C. Maxwell**

https://www.ramseysolutions.com/budgeting/how-to-take-control-of-your-money

"You can afford anything, but not everything." — **Paula Pant**

https://affordanything.com/about/

"The four most dangerous words in investing are: 'This time it's different.'" — **Sir John Templeton**

https://www.bakertilly.com/insights/this-time-its-different-investing-danger

"We simply attempt to be fearful when others are greedy and to be greedy only when others are fearful." — ***Warren Buffett***

https://www.berkshirehathaway.com/letters/1986.html

"Our favorite holding period is forever." — ***Warren Buffett***

https://www.berkshirehathaway.com/letters/1988.html

"The first rule of compounding is to never interrupt it unnecessarily." — ***Charlie Munger***

https://www.independentvanguardadviser.com/compounding-takes-time/

"The biggest risk of all is not taking one." — ***Mellody Hobson***

https://www.investopedia.com/financial-edge/0511/the-top-17-investing-quotes-of-all-time.aspx

"Invest in what you know." — ***Peter Lynch***

https://www.fidelity.com/learning-center/trading-investing/fundamental-etfs

"Never spend your money before you have it." — ***Thomas Jefferson***

https://www.monticello.org/encyclopedia/canons-conduct

Financial Industry Regulatory Authority. (2016). *Report on digital investment advice.* https://www.finra.org/sites/default/files/digital-investment-advice-report.pdf

Financial Industry Regulatory Authority. (2024). *Know your risk tolerance.* https://www.finra.org/investors/insights/know-your-risk-tolerance

Gathergood, J. (2012). Self-control, financial literacy and consumer over-indebtedness. *Journal of Economic Psychology, 33*(3), 590–602. https://doi.org/10.1016/j.joep.2011.11.006

Gollwitzer, P. M. (1999). Implementation intentions: Strong effects of simple plans. *American Psychologist, 54*(7), 493–503. https://doi.org/10.1037/0003-066X.54.7.493

Harkin, B., Webb, T. L., Chang, B. P. I., Prestwich, A., Conner, M., Kellar, I., Benn, Y., & Sheeran, P. (2016). Does monitoring goal progress promote goal attainment? A meta-analysis of the experimental evidence. *Psychological Bulletin, 142*(2), 198–229. https://doi.org/10.1037/bul0000025

Klontz, B., Britt, S. L., Mentzer, J., & Klontz, T. (2011). Money beliefs and financial behaviors: Development of the Klontz Money Script Inventory. *Journal of Financial Therapy, 2*(1), 1–22. https://doi.org/10.4148/jft.v2i1.451

Loewenstein, G. F., Weber, E. U., Hsee, C. K., & Welch, N. (2001). Risk as feelings. *Psychological Bulletin, 127*(2), 267–286. https://doi.org/10.1037/0033-2909.127.2.267

Madrian, B. C., & Shea, D. F. (2001). The power of suggestion: Inertia in 401(k) participation and savings behavior. *The Quarterly Journal of Economics, 116*(4), 1149–1187. https://doi.org/10.1162/003355301753265543

Matz, S. C., Gladstone, J. J., & Stillwell, D. (2016). Money buys happiness when spending fits our personality. *Psychological Science, 27*(5), 715–725. https://doi.org/10.1177/0956797616635200

Shim, S., Barber, B. L., Card, N. A., Xiao, J. J., & Serido, J. (2010). Financial socialization of first-year college students: The roles of parents, work, and education. *Journal of Youth and Adolescence, 39*(12), 1457–1470. https://doi.org/10.1007/s10964-009-9432-x

Soroka, S., Fournier, P., & Nir, L. (2019). Cross-national evidence of a negativity bias in psychophysiological reactions to news. *Proceedings of the National Academy of Sciences, 116*(38), 18888–18892. https://doi.org/10.1073/pnas.1908369116

Thaler, R. H. (1999). Mental accounting matters. *Journal of Behavioral Decision Making, 12*(3), 183–206. https://doi.org/10.1002/(SICI)1099-0771(199909)12:3%3C183::AID-BDM318%3E3.0.CO;2-F

Thaler, R. H., & Benartzi, S. (2004). Save More Tomorrow: Using behavioral economics to increase employee saving. *Journal of Political Economy, 112*(S1), S164–S187. https://doi.org/10.1086/380085

Van Boven, L., & Gilovich, T. (2003). To do or to have? That is the question. *Journal of Personality and Social Psychology, 85*(6), 1193–1202. https://doi.org/10.1037/0022-3514.85.6.1193

About the Author

Bruce Hoyt is the author of How Not To Suck At Managing Your Money: *Money by Design*. At 75 years old, Bruce Hoyt is busier than ever. He has over 40 years of top management experience and currently assists in running two different companies while also being CFO of an innovative software company and President of Four Aces Publishing LLC. He also has over 30 years of experience in stock trading and 6 years of experience in crypto trading. In his spare time, he enjoys taking RV trips, playing in poker tournaments and writing and publishing books in numerous categories. He holds a BS in Organizational Behavior from the University of San Francisco and an MBA from San Jose State University.

www.ingramcontent.com/pod-product-compliance
Lightning Source LLC
LaVergne TN
LVHW010738061126
851857LV00014B/1540
* 9 7 9 8 9 0 5 9 9 9 5 1 2 *